34A

CITY CATS OF ISTANBUL

Photographs by Marcel Heijnen
Haiku and cat stories by Ian Row

FOREWORD

by Fatih Dağlı

Founder of the Cat Museum Istanbul

This city is a wonderland for street photography. Layers of intricate architecture frame the daily lives of a diverse crowd, representing a rich blend of ethnicities and cultures. Capturing a 'still life on the streets' here would feel incomplete without the presence of Istanbul's most iconic resident – the street cat.

The growing awareness of Istanbul's street cats highlights an extraordinary reality: every day, millions of Istanbulites interact with, care for and help sustain hundreds of thousands of cats across this ancient city. And Marcel presents this unique connection in a poetic and creative way.

With his lens still warm from capturing shop cats in China, it was only a matter of time before Marcel would take his camera to Istanbul, our special city that is teeming with opportunities to photograph its street cats – and what a wonderful series these books have become!

As you turn each page, the harmony between images and the mounting curiosity for the next shot reveal Marcel's meticulous curation. Each photograph transports readers to a new part of the city, blending feline beauty with subtle glimpses of Istanbul's urban culture. Though no longer relied upon as protectors of grain stores and warehouses, the people's affection for cats remains steadfast. This book celebrates these cats and their enduring relationship with human caretakers, as they continue to grace the streets with countless photogenic poses.

TAKSi

HELLO KEDI!

by Marcel Heijnen

As a photographer, I've always been drawn to cities that pulse with life – places where history, culture and the everyday stories of people blend seamlessly into the urban landscape. My journey with cats started several years ago in Hong Kong, where I first began documenting the beautiful connection between felines and their environment. That work, which culminated in the photobooks *Shop Cats of Hong Kong* and *Shop Cats of China*, sparked an enduring fascination in me for the way people and animals coexist in cities.

So it was hardly a surprise that, after photographing cats in urban China, Istanbul was next on the list. What started as an exploration of the city and its famed cats ultimately turned into a layered love letter to a place that lives and breathes with the calm and graceful presence of these animals.

HYBRID CATS

The first time I set foot in Istanbul, I was immediately struck by the omnipresence of cats. They were everywhere, weaving themselves into the very soul of the city – perched on rooftops, lounging in café windows, darting between the legs of busy pedestrians or simply basking in the sun atop ancient ruins. I realized quickly that these weren't just 'strays' in the way we often perceive street animals. These were cats that belonged to the city in a way that was hard to put into words. They weren't just surviving in Istanbul – they were thriving, living harmoniously alongside the people who called the city home. The cats here are neither pets nor strays but rather a kind of hybrid. They aren't owned by their fellow Istanbulites, but they aren't left to their own devices either – the whole community takes care of them collectively.

It felt as though at every corner I turned, there was a new story waiting to be told. The orange tabby who had claimed a corner of a bustling spice market, seemingly unfazed by the daily chaos around him. In another neighbourhood, a slightly plus-sized calico lounged on the steps of an ancient mosque, blending into the warm hues of the marble. Istanbul's cats had no sense of boundaries; they wandered freely between worlds, from the historic grandeur of Ottoman architecture to the humble backstreets where laundry fluttered between crowded buildings. And everywhere they went, they were greeted with warmth and affection by the city's human residents, who regularly share their lunch with them.

That's what struck me the most: the relationship between the people and the cats wasn't one of indifference. It was one of mutual respect and, dare I say, love. I saw shopkeepers and other residents leaving out bowls of food and water, building small shelters for cats in alleyways and tourists stopping in their tracks to snap a photo or share a smile with a feline passerby. These cats were more than just animals on the street – they were part of the essence of daily life, cherished by the city in a way that felt almost sacred.

CAPTURING THE SPIRIT OF THE CITY

As I began photographing Istanbul's cats, I realized this project was as much about the city as it was about the cats themselves. Through my lens, I saw how these animals connected the city's past and present, traversing Istanbul's many worlds with ease and grace. One moment, I'd capture a cat perched regally atop an ancient lion sculpture, as if standing guard over the relics of the Byzantine era. The next, I'd find a kitten curling up on a café chair, seemingly right at home amidst the hum of modern life. The cats of Istanbul reflect the city's diversity, its contrasts and its constant state of flux. They roam the alleys of old neighbourhoods where time seems to have stood still, yet they also blend seamlessly into the bustling heart of the city where modernity reigns. It was this duality that I wanted to capture – the idea that these cats are not just wandering creatures but are living symbols of Istanbul's spirit.

A HISTORICAL SYMBIOTIC RELATIONSHIP

Cats were first domesticated around 9,000 years ago in the Fertile Crescent, a region that includes parts of modern-day Turkey, Syria, Iraq and surrounding areas. This likely occurred when wild cats were attracted to human settlements for food, and ended up helping control pests around stored grains. Over time, these cats developed mutually beneficial relationships with humans, laying the foundation for an even more symbiotic relationship to come.

The connection between Istanbul and its cats has deep historical roots as well. As a major port city, Istanbul was vulnerable to rats and other vermin that could spread diseases and damage food supplies. Cats, with their keen hunting abilities, were invaluable in controlling these populations, particularly in the bustling markets and port areas. Over time, their role as protectors of the city's health and safety became appreciated, and they were welcomed into public spaces. This relationship was both practical and symbolic: cats came to be seen as guardians of the home and community.

As Istanbul's importance grew during the Ottoman Empire, the cat population flourished along with it. Cats could be found everywhere, their presence so intertwined with the urban fabric that it was difficult to imagine the city without them. While their role as protectors may have diminished over the years, their place in Istanbul's history and identity endures.

CULTURAL AND RELIGIOUS REVERENCE

The prevalence of cats in Istanbul is also rooted in religious tradition. As a predominantly Muslim country, Turkey draws much of its affection for cats from Islamic teachings, in which cats are considered ritually clean animals. The Prophet Muhammad is said to have had a deep fondness for cats, and one of the most famous anecdotes describes how he once cut off a sleeve of his robe rather than disturb his sleeping cat, Muezza. This story, among many others, fosters respect and kindness towards cats in Muslim cultures.

In Istanbul, this religious reverence translates into everyday acts of care. It is common to see people leaving bowls of food and water outside their homes or shops for stray cats. Cats are also given shelter in mosques and other public spaces. In the courtyards of Istanbul's famous mosques, such as the Blue Mosque, it's not unusual to see cats lounging peacefully, often approached with gentle affection by worshippers. The teachings of Islam, combined with a strong sense of hospitality and responsibility towards the less fortunate, have ensured that cats are treated with respect and kindness.

A LEGAL NOTE

Laws protecting stray animals reflect Istanbul's commitment to humane treatment. The Animal Protection Law, first enacted in 2004 and amended in 2021, redefined animals as 'living beings', giving strays legal rights against cruelty and instituting penalties, including jail time, for harming them. This legal change was part of broader efforts to control the stray population humanely, primarily through sterilization and vaccination initiatives.

In 2024, however, new legislation aimed at addressing safety concerns shifted focus towards removing stray dogs from urban areas and housing them in shelters. Originally including cats, the law was revised to exempt them after public outcry – a demonstration of the exceptional position cats have in Turkish society. The legislation regarding dogs has sparked protests over potential risks of euthanasia due to funding constraints, and activists are pushing for sustainable and humane solutions that honor Istanbul's tradition of compassion for street animals. Let's see how this story develops.

CATS AS CULTURAL ICONS

Beyond their practical and symbolic roles, cats have also become cultural icons in Istanbul. They appear in local art, literature and even cinema. One notable example is the 2016 documentary *Kedi*, which gained international acclaim for its portrayal of the cats of Istanbul. The film follows several cats as they roam the city, offering a glimpse into their lives and interactions with the humans who care for them. *Kedi* showcases the unique place of cats in Istanbul's culture and highlights the affection and respect they receive from the city's residents. In fact, *Kedi* was released when I was working on my first book in the Chinese Whiskers series, the *Shop Cats of Hong Kong* book, and it inspired me a great deal.

HELLO KEDI

City Cats of Istanbul is more than just a collection of photographs. For me, it's an invitation to see the city through the eyes of its feline inhabitants – to witness the quiet moments of connection between human and animal life, to appreciate the way the past and present coexist in the city's streets and to understand the special bond that exists between Istanbul's people and its cats. Through these images, I want to share a piece of the magic that I experienced while working on this project. I hope to inspire others to look more closely at the world around them, to notice the quiet grace of animals living alongside us, and to appreciate the simple beauty of everyday life.

The cats of Istanbul have a way of reminding us that even in the busiest, most chaotic of places, there are always moments of stillness and connection waiting to be found. So, as you turn the pages of this book, I invite you to say 'Hello, Kedi' – to greet these cats as the residents of Istanbul do, with warmth, respect and a sense of wonder.

A NOTE ON THE HAIKU

The traditional (Japanese) haiku is made up of 3 lines and 17 sounds. Sounds in the Japanese language are not equivalent to syllables in English. For example, the word 'haiku' is two syllables in English (hi-ku), but three sounds in Japanese (ha-i-ku). So the 5–7–5 syllable rule is effectively a Western imposition and places excessive emphasis on form. What's essential in writing haiku is the development – some would say the 'unfolding' – of a story. The haiku in this book therefore pay homage to the traditional short-long-short format, as opposed to following a strict 5–7–5 structure, while staying true to the spirit of the poetic form.

MEKAP
SATIŞ NOKTASI
MEKAP
ÜNVER
Beybi

İMLER
YETKİLİ SATIŞ NOKTASI
TERAZİ-BASKÜL

Me: scratch me

Also me: yes, yes don't stop

You: I have a boyfriend

Man drifts, travels
Blessings and goodwill in gold leaf
Cat just waits

HAGIA SOPHIA
Istanbul
GODS OF NEMRUD
TAM
YERINDEN

First morning tea break

First of many reunions

Say ‘sardine!’

47
Erikli

Waiting and seeing

Weighing options and plotting routes

We set out in 10

Hayır

Your breakfast

My gift to you

A loan from God

SEVEN
BALIK MARKET
HOŞGELDINIZ
Tel.0216 346 6816

Closing shop

'Here, I saved this for you'

'It better be lamb'

Coca-Cola

A safe staircase
The people here must have food
The smell of promise

Where do they come from

A buzz of busy bodies

Nappus interruptus

KADIKÖY

CUBE

Spare some change

The ones that sing and those who sleep for a living

Weary cat contemplates
Would you pay more attention if
I made you money

Everyday, the same

His mind goes to dark places

I try to be light

Anonim
İSTANBUL

I'm new around here
The old man is good to me
And the food is fresh

I know this woman

My mother from a previous life

You always return

The water is fresh
Brotherhood has no boundary
Some gifts are priceless

First day, new job
I'm an ambassador!
When is lunch?

It’s a bird, it’s a plane

It’s Catman! No, it’s Batcat!

You know it makes sense

Warm summer's day

Humans swelter

The cat bakes

The indoor cat is out
Few hours to catch up on things
Life lived inside out

69
69

MADAME CAKI

The Cat at the Mosque

Good morning, good afternoon and good evening. I am Madame Caki, the resident cat at these premises. Let me explain to you what 'resident cat' means: it means I...am *home*. I know how blessed I am, to have all the creature comforts and privileges. One of those privileges is being able to pay it forward.

So, I'm up early every morning ready to greet everyone. *Anyone.* These days, most of them come with heavy hearts. I calm them down, get them to breathe and centre themselves before they go into the big house. *Come on people! Remember our breathing! We did this the last time! Focus. Focus!* Yes, that's what I do.

I take my duties very seriously and I often step in for the Imam if he's unavailable. Look, he can't be everywhere at once, so that's when I step up. Obviously not during prayers because I'm not *that* kind of cat! But I can hold your hand and give you a blessing. I want to be there for people. I'm very much a people person.

MADAME CAKI

MADAME CAKI

Of all God's creatures
the cat is most cognizant
of its power

الله

A pat for good luck
Blessings for the family
Go well, my sister

Good to see you bro

You won't believe who's inside

Got your back (and mine)

Here for the vibes

The wide open spaces

The elevation

SERVET
KUAFÖR
SALONU

History is calling
Literally, at your feet
Shoulders of giants

Reporting for duty

A permanent straycation

It's a living

CAFER
KURU
TEMİZLEME
E

Wake up, Sunshine

Time to venture and conquer

But first, pray

VAKIFLAR

History repeats

The call of His Master's Voice

Memory summoned

"His Master's Voice"

I woke up like this

Beauty and the Baggage

Keeping it real

I’m trying to sleep
I said, I’m trying to sleep
Going back to sleep

His furry ears

an antenna to decipher

your sweet nothings

HAN
ŞABAN
POLAT

My precious baby
Your eyes a new dimension
Tell me what you see

There are these rumours
that it was ‘based on a true story’
No one believes that

That shifty moment
when object becomes subject
It’s your story now

LOLA

The Cat at the Leather Shop

I'm Lola. I live here. It was me and mama for as long as I could remember – then one day, she was gone. It's been a couple of years since, but it's still an odd thing to say out loud. I'm an only child. Just sayin'. I'm also not lonely. Just putting it out there. Anyway, now it's me and Ali. Or Boss, as I call him. Ali says it's ironic that he gets called 'Boss' when it's me who's truly running the household. No comment.

But oh, we have a great set up here! As you can see, the retail shop is very stylish – it's textured, the lighting is good. There's form, function. The workshop is at the back and that's where you'll find Boss in his element, using his hands to make things of beauty. Everyone should try that. I myself am quite 'hands on' and clearly I'm doing my visual merchandising thing. Boss says I'm getting a feel for the work – *meow!* – which, I have to say, is not particularly demanding or challenging. But it does get boring really quickly, and I have a short attention span. So some napping occurs. Often spontaneously. And on a regular basis.

LOLA

LOLA

Our lives so far

One long nap, with dreams and moments

A life slept well

Unaware

of a lineage of greatness

The child, unafraid

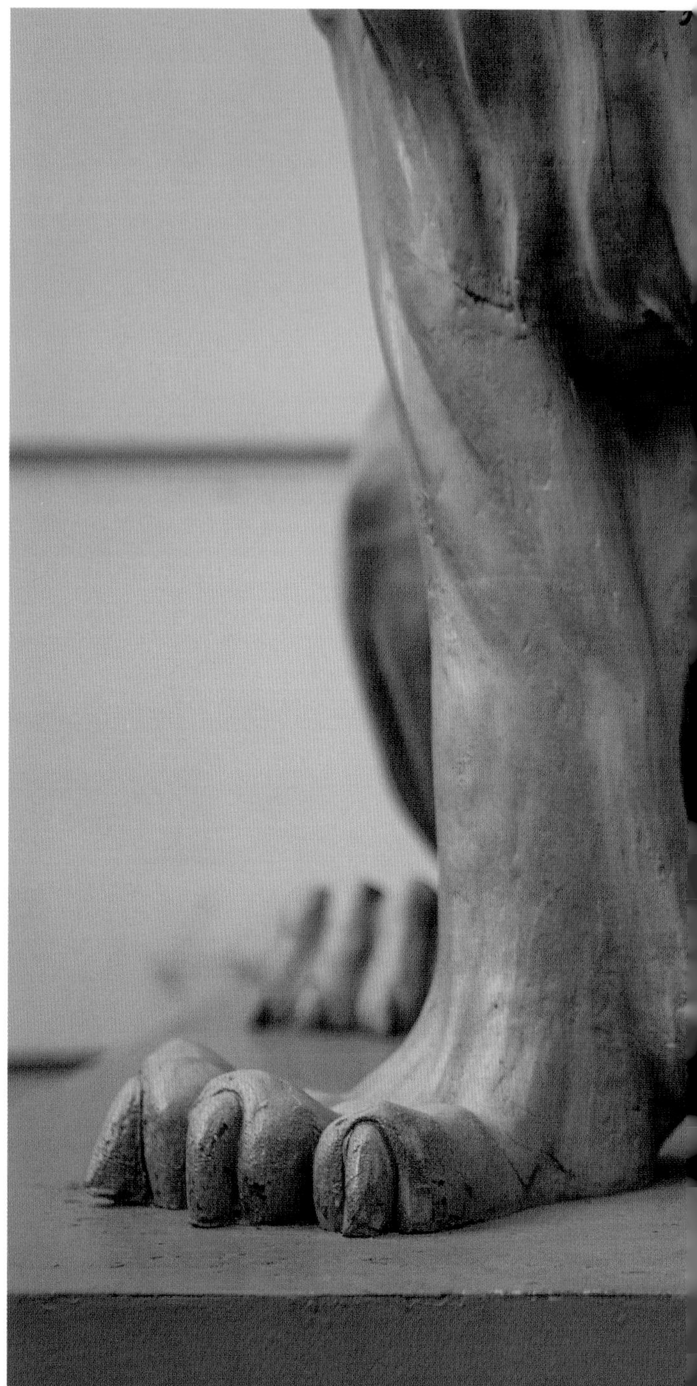

Where are you from

I hear it's fancy out there

Take me with you

Easy companions

A friendship of concessions

Love and let love

I’m here now

Not planning on being here later

I’m not telling

Copa Copacabana

You have no imagination

No cha cha for you

For the last time

I am not your father

Ask your mother

Profile: Romeo

I like late nights and long looks

Let's make some music

ORJINAL
9 TAŞ & 12 TAŞ

Yeah she works here

But if you want actual help

She'll get the man

CAFE
BİZİMLE
ÇALIŞMAK
İSTER MİSİNİZ ?
149
399
199,99
KART 220
kazara

Rest stop number 5
The fountain yields a few more laps
Ten thousand cat steps

A little madness

Don’t knock it until you try it

Home is where the head is

135

What’s your budget?

Big impressions cost big money

Love costs money

LIRA

The Cat from the Bank

I know what you're thinking – what's a cat like me doing in a place like this? Truth is, a number of my regulars work in this building, so I'm almost guaranteed something to eat if I'm at the right place at the right time. Are people who work in a bank more generous than people who don't work in a bank? Great question... Next!

A million dollars? What *would* a cat do with a million dollars?! I can't imagine it. I can't even count to a hundred. But I'm thinking the obvious – more investment in the National Cat Health and Wellbeing Plan; extend free public transport to all 81 provinces; and roll out a national 'Meals on Wheels' program for cats living rough. Clearly I've thought about this.

The reality is, money doesn't hold the same meaning for us cats in the way it does for people. I know how it works, I've seen what it can do. I've also seen what it does to people. So I like to keep it simple: share what you have and take care of each other. My name? It's Lira.

LIRA

Everything we need –
close your mouth when you cough –
is here

Prepare for takeoff!
A cat on a flying carpet
Who would believe it?

I see a boy band
With the right representation
they could go far

I’m new

What are you?

What is ‘cute’?

Sevim Ak
Sevim Ak

Uzm. Dr. Ece Balkuv
BEYNİNİZ HAYATINIZI NASIL ŞEKİLLENDİRİR?
GABRIEL GARCIA MARQUEZ
YÜZYILLIK YALNIZLIK
ÇOCUKLAR ve KADINLAR
ŞEYMA DEMİR
FİNK
SERHAT

Older than I look

And younger than I feel

I’m worlds apart

Too young to worry

Am I pretty enough for this world?

Enough for me

MAİDE
FENER
FENER CAFE

Not again

This is not what I ordered

Two stars for you

KFC

19
RAM.REACH
SEMUR 3

Nothing to see
Okay, that's close enough
I don't wanna cuddle

Big city dreams

She wants to be a dancer

A ballerina

Something in the air

They think ‘oh no, this won’t end well’

But they’re ready

ARORA
Cappuccino 125
ARORA

Late night lights

A sky full of promise

A forever home

Ian Row was born and raised in Singapore and now lives in Melbourne, Australia. He has written haiku since 2006, when he realized how useful the form was in helping him to exist in the present moment. He now writes a blog called Hot Cross Haiku.

Marcel would like to thank Ian Row for revealing glimpses into cats' minds, Fatih Dağlı for the lovely foreword, Nadir Mehadji for coining the 'Hello Kedi' title, Cansu van Gageldonk, Aysha Raja and Steve Embrey for advice, cultural insights and encouragement and last but not least Amanda Tse for being a partner in life and all things feline.

First published in the United Kingdom in 2025 by
Thames & Hudson Ltd, 6–24 Britannia Street, London WC1X 9JD

First published in the United States of America in 2025 by
Thames & Hudson Inc., 500 Fifth Avenue, New York, New York 10110

www.marcelheijnen.com
Instagram: @chinesewhiskers

Haiku and stories by Ian Row, Instagram: @ianrow_hotcrosshaiku
Foreword by Fatih Dağlı, Cat Museum Istanbul, www.catmuseum.co
Essay by Marcel Heijnen
Author photograph by Amanda Tse

EU Authorized Representative: Interart S.A.R.L.
19 rue Charles Auray, 93500 Pantin, Paris, France
productsafety@thameshudson.co.uk
interart.fr

A CIP catalogue record for this book is available from the British Library

ISBN 978-0-500-29841-1
01

Printed and bound in China by 1010 Printing International Ltd